MW00677467

How to Have a Happy Childhood

Marianne Gingher

ZUCKERMAN CANNON PUBLISHERS

ISBN 0-9664316-1-8

*Please see the last page in the book for credits
and acknowledgments*

Manufactured in Korea

To my wonderful mother and father

Betty Jane and Rod Buie

Who taught me that a happy childhood

can last a lifetime

AND

To parents everywhere

Who do all that they can to bring up

strong, resilient, resourceful

and loving children

CR

If you want to

have a happy childhood,

observe all the

opportunities that

tumble

out of surprise.

Look closely in the shadows

for the palest indications

that there is more to

every story, more to every person,

more, always, to know.

CR

*D*on't let happiness see you lurking around
with nothing to do.

*K*eep busy while happiness skips all around.
If you play hide-and-seek with it,
happiness will hide
and you will have to find it.
You might accidentally bump into it
while looking elsewhere.

*P*lay outdoors a lot. Go
bare-footed in the summer—
it's the only way to feel
the heartbeat of the earth. Keep
a lookout for something shy
or rare: a hummingbird,
a fawn, a box turtle,
a May-apple, a
Jack-in-the-
Pulpit.

It helps
to have brothers or sisters
or a mix of both.
They will test your tolerance and humanity
better than friends
because you can't get away from them.

If you can be happy with them,
you will be learning how to be happy
with anyone.

You must learn to survive
the claustrophobia
of their heckling inconvenience.
They will perplex and embarrass you,
cheat you, betray you,
harangue you and
occasionally comfort you.
They can be fiercely jealous
or fiercely proud of you.

Of all the people in the world,
brothers and sisters know just how far
to bend back your fingers
without popping the bones
out of joint.

*M*ake a pal
out of somebody who isn't a
bit like you:
the hurried postman,
a grouchy cleaning lady,
the retired elderly couple
who moves into
your neighborhood
and who used to perform
as trapeze artists.

*A*sk your parents to tell you all they can remember
about their childhoods. Be greedy for family history,
even the stories that you've heard your father tell
so many times the details are fuzzy because
you've often tuned him out.

*H*is stories have been like beehives you've
been required to stick your head into, and
the words have buzzed
all around you, a droning muddle.
You've endured them,
but you haven't allowed them to penetrate
and niche.

*L*isten to the worn out stories one more patiently,
gleaning time and, like an historian, write the stories
in a notebook so that they can't be lost. Nobody
will write them down if you don't.

*A*nd do write them down.
Practice your penmanship. Sign your name with a
flourish, like the men who signed the Declaration of
Independence. Never become so sober-minded and
responsible that you can't be theatrical, as well.

Go speeding on your bicycle.
Experience the exultant, lacy taste of snowflakes.
Rock-a-bye your favorite doll and
smell the bronze scent of her waxy hair.

Dare yourself, not somebody else,
to go wobbling on tall stilts,

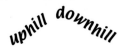

in a slow glissando of thrill.

Watch the quarter moon,
dippering over a pond pontooned
with lily pads, frogs afloat on them,
singing their grumpy arias.
You will know another kind of
happiness then, solitary,
transcendent, almost divine.

*A*sk your parents to show you things
they were taught to do as children.
Pay close attention to the process of how such things
are done. You have more time for learning
complicated processes and tricks when you are young,
and, later, there might not be anyone around
who can teach you how to thread an old
treadle sewing machine or weave
Crow's Feet with a piece of looped string
or how to roll out a pie crust
or bake a meringue or sing a song
from some distant decade.

♫

You will be brought
happiness years later
remembering the vain little toad
who donned his opera hat
and went 'a courtin' to
Miss Mousie's hall,
and how your parents sang
the whole epic song with you,
as if they had all the
time in the world.

♫

Observe the air's hymn and filigree
of insects. Close up
they resemble a combination of
minute engines, monsters, toys.
Watch for a swarm of bees woven
as tightly together as a bushy brown
doormat suspended from the branch of a tree.
A black widow spider, cruel as a tack,
creeps across her web on stiletto legs.

DON'T KILL HER.
Smashing something you fear
is always less illuminating
than learning to live in proximity
with its tiny wicked strategies.

*F*ind a shady spot and lie down beside your
smiling dog. His eyes shine the moist color of calm—
kindly and deep and brown as mud—
imprinted with your happiness.
There is nothing pinker on earth than
his flapping, silly tongue, nothing crustier than the pads
of his paws. His breath is luxuriantly rank and steamy.
Bump heads with him and transfer dreams.

*H*old your cat in your lap while it sleeps.
Modern cats are *jumpier* than in the past
because nobody sits still long enough
to wallow in their lull. But some days a child can sit still
for a thousand years—couldn't you, drowsy with
sensation? Stroking the furry keyboard of ribs, you'll feel a
flutterance of percussion. Your palms and fingers attend and
beseech the gift of softness, like turning a favor into silk.

Be resourceful

Make your own Mother's
or Father's Day cards.

Whenever you peer into a flip-top box of
64 brand-new unpeeled Crayola Crayons,
bow to Her Majesty, the Red Crayon, with her
perfect snobbery of a point.

Ride your bike every place it's feasible to go.

Figure out a way to construct a teepee
and stand one in your own backyard.
You'll need sturdy, long sticks
and old blankets.
If you use a red blanket
on a sunny day,
the light inside the teepee will be pink.

Build a campsite in the woods, although chances are it will be raided by the **neighborhood bully**—and there will always be a neighborhood bully. Rebuild your campsite every time he (or she, that unusually mean girl who seems to have it in for you) wrecks it.

When your parents go out for the evening and leave you with the **old sourpuss babysitter**, instead of the twinkly teenager one who enjoys your games, *devise your own safari.* If you don't have an attic, dark with box loads of mystery, then pretend that the kitchen counter-tops are cliffs or mountain tops.
Scale them in your bare feet.

Crouch atop the refrigerator like a bird of prey.

Swing open the tallest cabinets and dig for treasures inside the caves of shelves. You'll scavenge delicacies you never thought about eating until now: squares of bitter baking chocolate you can sprinkle with confectioner's sugar, Jell-O powder you can spoon right out of the box, dull citric swigs of your father's Tom Collins mixer, stale marshmallows you can try to revive over the glowing burner on your mother's range.

$\mathcal{K}$now all the names of
your neighbors
and wave to people in their yards
as you ride past on your bike.

Explore your neighborhood;

figure out every short cut.

Draw an explicit map

of your sidewalks and streets.

It may come in handy if you ever
come down with amnesia.

Give special names to the woods
and empty fields and the creeks where you play.
Hunt salamanders. Construct dams over the
narrow portions of streams. Make boats out of leaves
and put bugs in the boats for passengers.

Wade
in the creeks.
Tightrope across fallen logs.
It will be a rare day that you
don't fall in.
In wintertime if you lose your balance,
you will have to run home
in stinging, frozen jeans and
undress in the utility room
and bundle in a warm bathrobe and thaw out
over a heat grate while holding
a cup of hot chocolate.

Play in the summer rain,
fully dressed, as often as you're allowed.

Look out for drowning earthworms
that float to the surface of yards during
a downpour;
try to save as many as you can.
It's like plucking wrinkles from the
grass.

Go away to summer camp
before the age of 12 in order to experience
the clamorous pangs of homesickness—it
feels like starvation and thirst,
like your heart is an empty canteen
dropped into an emptier canyon.

Become the master of bluffs, booby-traps,
brags, dares, and Whoopee cushions
strategically placed.

Become *blood kin*
with someone you
like and invent secret codes,
passwords, aliases
and nicknames.

*L*earn to jump from the jungle gym
and roll wildly in the dust like a bucked off buckaroo.
Understand the glamour of dirt
the way your older sister
understands make-up, your mother, finesse.

Always wish on stars
and birthday candles
and single shoes left in the road.
Make up a story about
how in the world a person could lose
only one shoe.

*T*hink about how words are born.
For instance, shouldn't the word *cherish*
come from cherry? Imagine the dewy ruby sight
of a frosty jar of cherries, puckering in
the mellow light of the refrigerator like a
preserve of valentines.

Tell ghost stories at slumber parties.
Tell about maggots and fingernails as long as spikes
and chopped off toes that keep on walking
and goulash made from guts.
Peel grapes and put them in a paper sack
and force your friends to stick their hands
into the sack to touch the **freshly
harvested eyeballs.**

If you put a flashlight in your mouth
and close your lips around it, your cheeks
will be filled with a
glowing blood color
that will also beam out of your nostrils.

Learn to work a Ouija board
by the time you are ten.
Light a candle and hold a séance on a
rainy night with one or two good friends.

Don't be afraid to poke a dead animal,
to stir its immense stillness into
captive mystery. Tilt the livid feathers
of a dead starling and watch
of rainbow shimmer
across the wing.

If a stray follows you,
take care of it, or find it a good home.
Become, for a little while,
a stray yourself. Locate that rare
undeveloped patch of woods near
your house and try earnestly
to get lost in it.

Search out wild blackberry thickets
and, in June, when the berries ripen,
eat them right off the vine.
There may be little brown ants on them
that taste like pine resin.

Suck honeysuckle flowers
and eat four-leaf clovers for good luck.
Fill your mouth with the giddy
tilt-a-whirl flavors of wood sorrel.
Chewing mint leaves will make your
mouth feel like an echo.

⌘

$\mathcal{M}$ake mud pies and decorate them
with nandina berries,
but don't flinch
when a daddy long legs
wisps across your arm like a fringe—
they aren't spiders.

On your birthday,
ask your mother to bring
you breakfast in bed.
On her birthday,
make her breakfast and
deliver it to her
on a silver tray along with the
unfurled newspaper.

*Keep a diary
with a lock.*

$\mathcal{H}$ave a best friend
and love her for how she brings
out the best in you.

*I*f you decide to tell somebody
in your family that you're sorry
for something you did,
but it's late and everyone's in bed,
write a note of sincere apology,
fold it and deposit it in that person's
shoe before you go to sleep.

*I*f you ever have to move away
from the house you've lived in
since the day you were born,
write a letter to the house
and fill it with good memories,
then bury the letter
in the deepest innards of the attic
or basement for the house to keep forever.
You will be giving happiness
to the person who finds it.

*A*llow your grandmother to spoil you,
no matter how your parents fret.
Hope, when you visit her and open her refrigerator,
you'll find chilled six-ounce Cokes
in stout green bottles and chocolate
cream pie waiting just for you.

*Y*our grandmother will show you
how to do all the things your mother
may be too busy to show you, slower things,
like polishing slender knives,
graceful spoons and the fingers of forks
with Wright's Silver Cream.
She will teach you the rules for Dominoes,
Parcheesi and Crocinole, but you'd better learn
the following games as well: Go Fish,
Crazy Eights, Gin Rummy, Hearts,
Five-Card-Draw Poker, Casino,
Oh Hell and Spit.

Your brothers will want

to play

Fifty-Two Card Pickup,

but don't agree to it or

you'll be

the one picking up

all the

cards they fling into

the air.

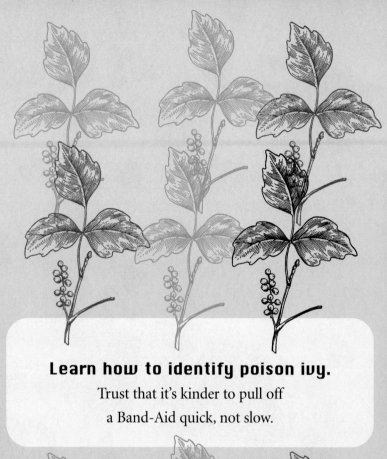

Learn how to identify poison ivy.

Trust that it's kinder to pull off
a Band-Aid quick, not slow.

Consider your summer successful if,
day after day,
you didn't step on a single bee
while whizzing your barefooted way around the corner
and down a block, racing to play with your best friend,
taking the short cut, faster than your bike, not paying
a bit of attention to your churning feet as
they propel you through the humming
red chenille of clover.

Don't

only read mysteries when real ones
dart and settle into the shadows just beyond your
own yard. Consider why the elderly woman
across the street always rolls her trashcan to the
curb after midnight. Why does the man next
door sit on the bumper of his car after supper
and smoke a cigar? What is he plotting?
What caused the dark spots on the concrete floor
of his garage—**oil or blood?**
Attach yourself to your favorite mystery
and try to solve it.

Lie

on your stomach someplace comfortable
with good light and something tasty to eat—
an apple salved with peanut butter, a
tangerine to peel, pretzels twinkling
with studs of salt—
and read way past your bedtime.

Read

The Secret Garden,
The Boxcar Children, *Call of the Wild,*
all the Nancy Drews you can find,
the Tarzan books, *Bartholomew
and the Oobleck,* Roald Dahl,
mythology, Grimm Brothers' fairy tales,
Andrew Lang's, Uncle Wiggily books,
the Wizard of Oz series, all of them,
Hans Christian Andersen's stories—
although some of them are sad,
folk tales from around the world,
poetry by Walter de la Mare, Aesop,
Mother Goose rhymes, Edward Lear
and Lewis Carroll, *Wind in the Willows,*
Jack tales from the Appalachian
mountains, and all that
Lois Lenski ever wrote.

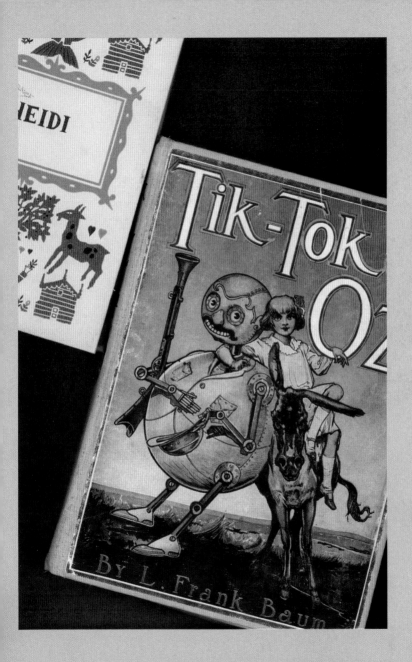

*A*nd
you need to have a
Southern relative who can read you
Uncle Remus without stumbling
over the briar-patch grammar
and who knows all the parables
of the Bible by heart
and can quote
the King James version.

Pray for luck
in your life,
because luck and happiness
are not the same thing.
Nobody can teach you how to
have luck.

*I*magine that happiness is a
freshly planted field. Above the field,
the kaleidoscopic weather swirls.
Suddenly, somebody accidentally tumbles
out of a plane, and at the last,
survivable second,
a parachute blooms in the sky.
You would have seen luck, then,
falling from the sky towards a happy ending.

*H*ardest of all—and luckiest:
be born to parents who admire
and *cherish* one another.
They are the King and Queen of your
childhood, and their own happiness will
anoint you like the radiance
from golden crowns.

*I*f they fuss occasionally, remember that
some arguments exist to define
distinctions between people.

Υour parents will kiss and hold hands
in front of you more often than they argue.
Observe how your father embraces
your mother
and tilts her backwards until
she lets go of the spoon
with which she's been stirring something
on the stove, and the baby stops fussing,
the clock stops, maybe time,
and even the irreverent sausage stops
sizzling in the pan.

As the wind curling around the house
quiets for their kiss,
you are holding your breath, too,
watching them silently
promise you an ever-after, glimpsing
what happiness looks like
when it's grown.

END

ꙮ Acknowledgments

 photo courtesy of FPG International

 photo courtesy of PhotoDisc

The following photos courtesy of of the Giduz Collection, North Carolina Collection, University of North Carolina Library at Chapel Hill

The balance of the illustrations used are from private collections.

This book was designed and produced by Kachergis Book Design Pittsboro, North Carolina